THE
SUSTAINABLE
PLASTICS
ECONOMY

Teresa Clark
teresa.clark@ensoplastics.com

THE   SUSTAINABLE   PLASTICS
ECONOMY

TERESA CLARK

The Circular Economy was created from the idea that we can create sustainable human systems by mimicking the sustainable processes in nature. A methodology to ensure resources flow continually between systems, where the waste from one process becomes a resource for another.

The Sustainable Plastics Economy adopts this philosophy and creates a system without plastic waste that can ultimately integrate into nature, and most importantly can be implemented by organizations immediately.

Overview

In nature, there is no such thing as waste. A simple observation of any ecological environment will indicate how resources flow between systems. A simplistic illustration of resource flows would be: The grass absorbs the suns energy and minerals from the soil, the rabbit eats the grass to extract the energy, the fox consumes the rabbit to utilize the energy and when the fox dies, insects and microscopic organisms digest the fox to claim the energy until finally it is returned to the soil and the nutrients can be used again by the grass.

These "resources" take many forms, energy, minerals, plants, animals, microbes, water, sunlight and more. Every living organism that has existed on this planet has extracted and utilized the same resources, and then ultimately returned the resources for use by another living organism. This continual cycling of resources has supported life on this planet for thousands of years.

In human industrial systems, many resources flow one direction. From resource, to use and finally disposal as waste; we extract fossil fuel and use it to create energy and plastics, the plastics are used and then discarded into a landfill.

Over the decades this single direction trajectory has been business as usual. Industry extracts fossil fuels, mines metals, harvests plants with a single task in mind - create products to sell. There is little concern for the value of that material after use. Where nature creates circular processes, we have focused on linear ones. This disconnect between human and natural systems is creating an unsustainable system that could affect the very ability of this planet to sustain life, and is the genesis of the Circular Economy movement.

The Circular Economy was created from the idea that we, as humans, can utilize and restore resources by mimicking the circular flows within nature. That minerals, organics and other resources can be extracted, used to manufacture products, and then after use these products can be a valuable resource to either make new products or return to nature.

The overarching concept is to keep resources flowing and prevent waste. The continual flow of the Circular Economy applies to all resources, including plastics.

In the plastic industry, the Circular Economy is often mistaken for a rebranding of the "recycling agenda", however this would be a gross underestimation of the Circular Economy precept. Recycling is typically understood as using a waste product to manufacture a similar product; such as using discarded water bottles to manufacture new water bottles.

The primary focus of recycling is for plastic to remain in a continual cycle of use and recycling. The idea being that once a plastic is created, it should never be destroyed. This interpretation follows the traditional approach of increasing plastic recycle rates without addressing the technical limitations of the material. It also lacks the vision and robustness of the Circular Economy.

The Sustainable Plastics Economy is a new development that integrates a complete Circular Economy approach with the unique challenges of plastic. It includes the concepts of Sustainable Materials Management by addressing the full LCA impact of various plastic options such as, what types of materials to select, where to source raw ingredients, waste infrastructures, and customary discard scenarios.

The Sustainable Plastics Economy creates a dynamic, data driven approach to create a system designed to replicate and ultimately integrate into nature, as intended in the Circular Economy precept.

This guide provides an overview of the Circular Economy concepts and introduces the Sustainable Plastics Economy. Also included is guidance for organizations to implement the Sustainable Plastics Economy in a practical and pragmatic method.

Understanding the Circular Economy

The Circular Economy is a concept built on the principles of natural systems, wherein all resources are continually cycled. In nature, this process of resource cycling has continued for millions of years and is the crux of sustainability of life on this planet.

Every single atom of matter and energy is conserved, recycling over and over, infinitely. Substances change form and move from one type of molecule to another, but their constituent atoms never disappear. One of the most important atoms in natural systems is carbon – the building block of life.

All living and previous living plants and creatures are made primarily of carbon. They are considered "carbon based" or "organic". In this guide, it is referred to as "carbon based".

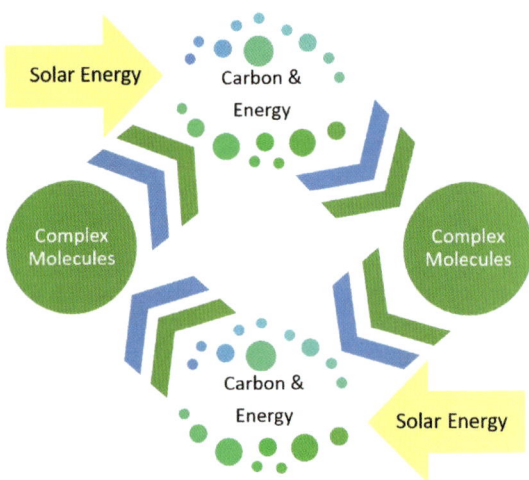

Solar Energy

Carbon & Energy

Complex Molecules

Complex Molecules

Carbon & Energy

Solar Energy

For carbon based materials, the carbon is formed into complex molecules (cells, organs, animals, plants), at death these molecules are deconstructed to utilize the energy within the molecular structure (when it is eaten by another organism), and then used to recreate complex molecules again (the digested carbon is used to build new cells, organs, etc.).

The actual flow of carbon becomes even more complex as it includes carbon moving from a solid state to a gas and then back again to a solid. Carbon flows involve a continual process of construction and destruction that have occurred from the beginning of life on this planet.

Each time the carbon changes forms it involves energy. Building molecules consumes energy and deconstructing them releases energy (often the release of energy is in the form of heat, so external energy is required to continue the cycle). If carbon is the building block of life, energy is the force that makes it possible. Without energy, all life would come to a screeching halt.

As you can see, the circular system of carbon is not an isolated environment -it requires external resources such as energy. Due to the laws of thermodynamics, carbon cycling requires continuous input of energy (luckily the sun provides an ample amount of energy!). Plants capture solar energy and pass it through the entire carbon system. The system of carbon cycling and energy has continued throughout the existence of life on this planet.

Interestingly, many of our modern "resources" are carbon-based, including fuels, pesticides, pharmaceuticals, plastics and more. These items all have value and a solution in the Circular Economy.

Let's consider for a moment the example of a cherry tree often used in Circular Economy literature, where it states that human systems should "act in the same way as a living system like the Cherry Tree in using all of the materials for new growth in an unending cycle."

It is often said that the devil is in the details. In sustainability, the solution is also in the details.

Let's look at the details of the cherry tree life. The cherry tree utilizes resources from the sun, soil, water and air to grow (create the complex molecules we discussed earlier), this includes roots, trunk, leaves, fruit

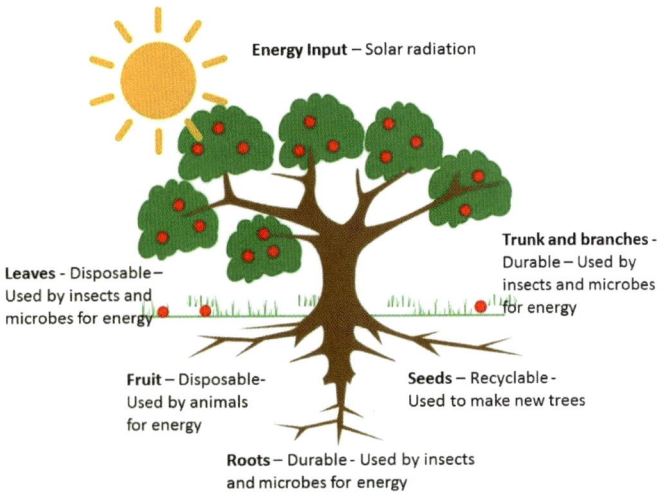

Energy Input – Solar radiation

Trunk and branches - Durable – Used by insects and microbes for energy

Leaves - Disposable – Used by insects and microbes for energy

Fruit – Disposable- Used by animals for energy

Seeds – Recyclable - Used to make new trees

Roots – Durable - Used by insects and microbes for energy and seed. Without the constant input of these external resources, the tree would die, and the cycle would end. Luckily, this has not been a problem and the tree has continued to grow. So we know that the tree requires external resources, and that the tree makes many different types of materials (branches, trunk, leaves, fruit, roots, etc..), but how is this part of a circular system?

The different parts of a cherry tree and how they fit into a circular system:

Root and Trunk: This part of the tree is intended to remain in use for decades. Ultimately when it is no longer needed (the tree dies), this material of complex molecules is deconstructed by other living organisms (insects, fungus, microbes) when they consume it as a form of energy. That energy is then used to sustain life (which releases carbon dioxide, a gaseous form of carbon used by plants) and create new and different types of carbon molecules. Ultimately, those organisms will also die, and the carbon will continue to flow.

Leaves: The leaves are made up of complex molecules but are designed for short term use. When they are discarded they fall to the ground and similar to the trunk and roots are deconstructed by other living organisms (animals, insects, microbes) to obtain energy for use in constructing new molecules.

<u>Fruit:</u> The fruit of the cherry is the packaging for the cherry seed. It is made up of complex molecules constructed only to package the seed and maximize the environment and opportunity for the seed to develop into a new cherry tree. The fruit, just as in the previous examples, is a complex molecule that is used by other organisms (animals, insects, fungus, microbes) for energy.

ENERGY OR TREES?

The growing of new plants from various parts of the plant is possible due to modern technology and understanding.

We can take the branches and create new trees using hormones, or take the DNA and use it to create new trees in the lab.

However, this is contrary to the natural cycles and is very inefficient.

Nature has already determined the highest value for each part of the tree. The seed grows a new tree and the remainder of the tree becomes resources for another system.

Growing plants from these sources removes the resource that these materials provide for other systems. It also requires significantly more resources than growing the tree from a seed.

So, while it is possible to force new scenarios, and try to make all parts of the tree grow new trees, it is not sustainable.

A wise rule of sustainability is:

Just because you can, doesn't mean you should.

<u>Seed:</u> The seed is the only part of the cherry tree that will be "recycled" into a new tree. It is a very small portion of the entire "Cherry Tree Economy". However, it is essential and valuable as it leads to the continuation of the existence of cherry trees (sustainability).

The value in the seed is in its ability to create a new tree. It could be used by organisms for energy, but the greater value is for the seed to make a new tree.

Energy or Trees? Most of the resources of the tree (root, trunk, leaves, fruit) are used by other organisms for energy, while a very small fraction (the seed) is valuable to create a new tree.

The best possible use for each part of the tree has been determined by evolution over millions of years to create the most efficient process for maintaining sustainability of a species – seeds to create trees and the remainder of the "tree economy," fallen leaves, dead branches or trunk to provide energy into the larger system that maintains the environmental conditions to sustain the future growth of new cherry trees.

As we apply the concepts of the cherry tree to plastic in the Circular Economy, one must remember that all plastics are carbon based molecules. What does this mean? Plastics are made of the same carbon atoms as all organic matter, including the cherry tree. To create a circular economy with plastics, we must use the carbon cycle found in nature as a template and the carbon in the plastic must ultimately become part of the carbon cycle of the planet. This is the overall objective of the Circular Economy and the result of the Sustainable Plastics Economy.

From a circular system perspective, it is easy to see that the cherry tree is part of a complex system. It is not as simple as using a tree and its resources to create a new cherry tree. The complexity of the system makes it robust, resilient and sustainable.

Building The Sustainable Plastic Economy

The Sustainable Plastics Economy is built to replicate the flow of resources within nature while accounting for material, infrastructure and economical limitations. It is a data driven program desinged to provide immediate value and environmental benefit. The Sustainable Plastics Economy is intended to be implemented immediately by most organizations with minimal cost implications while integrating into the existing waste infrastructures.

As in the overview of the Circular Economy, we will stay with the cherry tree analogy. Similar to the diversity of materials that comprise a cherry tree, plastics offer a variety of forms and compositions. In the Sustainable Plastics Economy, the diversity of materials is considered

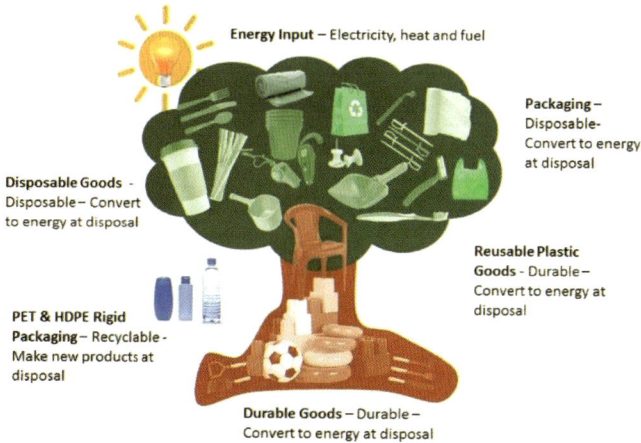

Energy Input – Electricity, heat and fuel

Packaging – Disposable - Convert to energy at disposal

Disposable Goods - Disposable – Convert to energy at disposal

Reusable Plastic Goods - Durable – Convert to energy at disposal

PET & HDPE Rigid Packaging – Recyclable - Make new products at disposal

Durable Goods – Durable – Convert to energy at disposal

critical and the end of life for each material is used at its greatest value.

Let's review the diversity of plastic products and how they relate to the cherry tree analogy.

Seeds Plastics that are recycled into new plastic products would be akin to a seed from the cherry tree. Mirroring the science of growing new tree with branches or roots, we can recycle all plastics. However, the resources required, and the resulting value does not make this a beneficial option. The primary materials that should be recycled are those that have the highest value for recycling.

Today, the plastics that demonstrate value, environmental and economic, are uncolored HDPE and PET bottles. These products can be considered the "seed" and should be recycled when possible to capture maximum value.

Leaves: The leaves are the disposable plastic products. They provide value for a short period of time but will be discarded without much reuse. There are many types of plastic that fall into this category and manufacturers should consider the performance requirements to provide maximum value. After use, just as leaves, these products should be recovered for energy value.

Branches and Roots: Plastics that are more durable and designed for long term use would compare to the branches and roots. These plastics should be designed for maximum durability to provide years of reuse. When these products are no longer reusable, they should be either recycled (if the LCA is favorable) or recovered for energy. In some instances, these products are favorable to recycle because there is a large amount of plastic in each item.

Fruit: People may love cherries, but packaging which is akin to the fruit is considered a planetary scourge. The sole purpose of packaging is to present, protect and transport a product.

For packaging, performance is the most important consideration – even above end of life. If a package is deficient, the entire product will become waste thus compounding the amount of overall waste. When packaging performs well, it extends the shelf life of perishables, prevents damage and breakage during transport, and provides an appealing presentation for products. Packaging should be designed to utilize as minimal amount of material without negatively affecting the performance. After use, a package should be discarded in a manner that recovers the energy value or when the LCA is favorable, recycled.

After use, recovery for energy is most often the highest value for plastics. Without energy, the entire plastics system will die, just like the cherry tree without energy from the sun.

BASIS OF THE SUSTAINABLE PLASTICS ECONOMY

The Sustainable Plastics Economy is based on the following 10 basic facts:

1. Plastic is a complex organic molecule. It can be made from fossilized or recently living plants – but it is simply organic molecules.

2. Choosing the right plastic for the job is the most sustainable. There are many forms of plastic used for many different purposes, if the wrong plastic is used simply because it has a better end-of-life option, it often causes substantially more waste than that of the plastic itself. This can be from reduced shelf life, product failure and lower performance.

3. Renewability and Sustainability are different. Full LCA analysis should be done to determine if the sourcing of a material is more sustainable than alternate sourcing.

4. Plastic cannot be recycled indefinitely. After 3-4 times of reprocessing, the plastic has become too weak to use and must be discarded. We will always need new materials.

5. Some forms of plastic are more environmentally and economically recycled. PET and HDPE rigid containers should be recycled when possible, other forms and types of plastic should be

discarded until the LCA of recycling the material proves beneficial.

6. Energy and plastic are inseparable. Plastic is a solid form of energy, all processing of plastic, transportation of plastic and use of plastic requires inputs of energy.

7. Discarded plastics should be recovered as energy. For many plastics, recovery of the energy is the most valuable opportunity. Energy recovery can be accomplished through landfill biodegradation, anaerobic digestion, incineration or other WTE technologies.

8. The more handling waste material requires, the higher the environmental and economic impact. Any handling of waste, including separation, transportation, cleaning, processing or conversion to energy will require inputs of resources. The most sustainable option is often the one that requires the least amount of handling.

9. The customary disposal of plastic is most important to end-of-life impact. Too often the focus is on niche disposal options or improper disposal of a small percentage of plastics. <u>The largest impact is in addressing the clear majority of plastic first</u>.

10. Data must lead all decisions. Popular trends, feel good tactics, consumer beliefs and marketing schemes do not dictate sustainability, all decisions should be based on facts, research and data.

The Sustainable Plastics Economy diagram combines the processes of plastic with the essential requirement of energy. By combining the material value with the energy value, we achieve a more robust and dynamic scenario. The Sustainable Plastics Economy Diagram is shown on the following page.

The Sustainable Plastics Economy

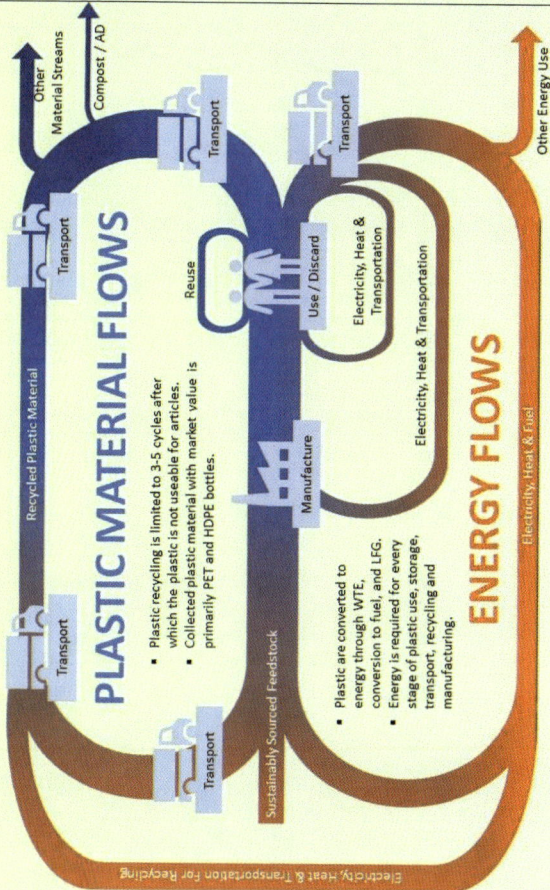

PLASTIC MATERIAL FLOWS

- Plastic recycling is limited to 3-5 cycles after which the plastic is not useable for articles.
- Collected plastic material with market value is primarily PET and HDPE bottles.

ENERGY FLOWS

- Plastic are converted to energy through WTE, conversion to fuel, and LFG.
- Energy is required for every stage of plastic use, storage, transport, recycling and manufacturing.

Transport

Recycled Plastic Material

Other Material Streams

Compost / AD

Reuse

Use / Discard

Electricity, Heat & Transportation

Manufacture

Electricity, Heat & Transportation

Sustainably Sourced Feedstock

Electricity, Heat & Fuel

Electricity, Heat & Transportation for Recycling

Other Energy Use

Key Aspects:

*Sustainability involves various aspects of a products life cycle, sourcing, use and discard. Circular Economy primarily focuses on end–of–life, whereas Sustainable Materials Management (SMM) has a more holistic approach. The Sustainable Plastics Economy encompasses both CE and SMM.

**In the circular economy, plastic and energy are integrally connected. Plastic is a solid form of energy, it requires energy to produce, transport and transform. At discard, plastic not recycled should be recovered as energy.

***SMM involves evaluating the entire life cycle impact, not simply the recycling/recovery aspect. Selecting plastic with optimal performance during use, can have greater benefits regardless of discard method. Sourcing should be evaluated for sustainability not simply renewability.

THREE PILLARS OF THE SUSTAINABLE PLASTICS ECONOMY

The Sustainable Plastics Economy is built on three basic pillars; sourcing, use and discard. Plastic is created from the most sustainable sources available, the right plastic is chosen based on physical properties required, and after use some of that plastic is recycled (when the LCA shows it is beneficial) while the remaining plastic is recovered as energy.

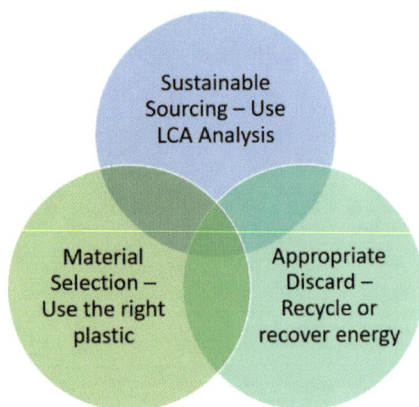

Sourcing:

To create plastic products both plastic material and energy are required inputs. It is not possible to create a plastic product without both material and energy.

Plastic systems will always require additional input, and will always have discards – that is one of the laws of physics. However, this should not be considered detrimental. All natural systems also have required inputs and discards.

The material inputs for plastic manufacturing can be sourced from renewable or fossil products. The Sustainable Plastics Economy position does not consider either source inherently superior.

The determination must be made by considering the full life cycle analysis of the various impacts; carbon footprint, water eutrophication, land use change, biodiversity impacts and human impacts.

Only after full analysis is complete can a determination be made if a specific material is best produced from renewable or fossil sources.

Material Selection:

The Sustainable Plastics Economy is based on the fundamental understanding that selecting the right plastic is fundamental to sustainability. The superior plastic is the one that performs most effectively.

Selecting a plastic with specific performance parameters will reduce product failure, increase shelf stability and prevent waste. This is especially true when considering plastics for packaging.

The environmental impact of the packaging is a small fraction of the impacts in creating the product itself. Failure of the package is nothing short of detrimental.

End-of-Life:

After a plastic product has fulfilled its intended use, that plastic should be discarded in a way to obtain maximum value. For specific plastics, such as rigid beverage containers, this means discarded into recycling systems that remanufacture new products.

Many other plastics, that have historically been considered "problematic", should be discarded into systems that recover the energy within the plastic.

Energy recovery can be accomplished in landfills, anaerobic digestion, incinerators or other energy conversion technologies.

Determination of the most appropriate method of discard must take into consideration the available infrastructure, economic impact, customary disposal and full life cycle analysis.

The Sustainable Plastics Economy is intended to support a sustainable waste infrastructure. The handling of waste (including recycling) is a business and should not require external governmental financial support.

Designing products with the appropriate discard in mind while properly educating consumers, will support a financially sustainable waste system.

The recycling of plastics is not a true end of life solution. Plastics can only be recycled 3-4 times before they are no longer useable. This means that while recycling is an important part of the Sustainable Plastics Economy, all plastics will eventually require permanent disposal.

The Sustainable Plastics Economy requires that plastic discards ultimately be converted into a form available for other systems, forms such as CO_2, CH_4, or other simple carbons. This will allow those carbons to integrate within the natural carbon cycle and ultimately be turned back into complex carbon molecules through a variety of natural processes.

5 STEPS TO A SUSTAINABLE PLASTICS ECONOMY*

1. Evaluate your exiting product material
2. Consider your product design.
3. Evaluate products disposal.
4. Support sustainability development.
5. Re-Evaluate your product

*See the summary for details on each step

FACTORS FOR SUSTAINABLE RECYCLING

Reports from recycling facilities demonstrate that in some regions, over 60% of materials placed in curbside bins for recycling are contaminants. Sorting facilities must spend additional money to collect and sort these contaminants while ultimately still disposing of them in a landfill.

Contamination in recycling is a direct effect on the environmental impact and economic sustainability of recycling. When only 40% of collected material is useable for recycling, it places a high burden on recycling facilities to remain profitable and requires significant energy and human resources.

The most important way a company can support recycling is to promote to their consumers the message of "only recycling the right items". This includes removing messages of recycling from packaging that should not be placed in curbside bins.

Placing recycling messages on products and materials that are not actively recycled is detrimental to the success of our recycling infrastructure. These messages encourage consumers to place additional burden on recyclers and the environment.

Summary

The Circular Economy is a principle of mimicking natural systems to replicate sustainability. The Sustainable Plastics Economy takes the principles of the Circular Economy and focuses it on plastics to create a robust, diverse and implementable program.

The Sustainable Plastics Economy is an understanding that we cannot isolate plastics in a closed system. Just as it is impossible to isolate a cherry tree and have it survive, sustainable systems are diverse, dynamic, and utilize data in making decisions.

The Sustainable Plastics Economy is designed to be implemented immediately with the following 5 steps:

1. Evaluate your exiting product to verify that you are using the best available material for your product – package and product failure must be minimized. Any failure or reduced stability will create additional waste.

2. Consider your product and package design. Can it be redesigned in a way that utilizes less resources, such as conversion from rigid to flexible multi-layer package. LCA shows that flexible packaging

is superior to rigid packaging even when considering recycling. *Be sure your decisions in step 2 do not negatively impact Step 1.*

3. Determine the customary disposal and take measures to maximize sustainability in this environment. Part of this is considering the ultimate end of life – how will the carbon return to the natural carbon cycle. ** *The D4D program by the Environmental Research and Education Foundation (EREF) can provide assistance and validation for this step.* www.erefdn.org/D4D

4. Once you have the right material, optimal design and integrate into your customary disposal, you can consider supporting new infrastructure, programs and future sustainability projects. This will provide continued improvement and technology while ensuring that the current state of your product has maximum sustainability.

5. Re-Evaluate your product on a periodic basis by repeating Steps 1-3 to account for changes in infrastructure, consumer behavior, product handling and new technologies that may affect the outcome of these steps.

The Sustainable Plastics Economy allows organizations to use data and science to make decisions leading toward sustainability. It is about allowing organizations to select the right material for the job and creating value from used products. Value that is useable in the plastic system as well as other natural systems.

THE SUSTAINABLE PLASTICS ECONOMY IS THE REPLICATION OF THE CARBON CYCLE IN NATURE, A SYSTEM THAT HAS BEEN SUSTAINABLE FOR MILLIONS OF YEARS AND WILL CONTINUE TO BE SUSTAINABLE LONG INTO THE FUTURE.

THE   SUSTAINABLE   PLASTICS
ECONOMY

TERESA CLARK

SAVE THE MOLECULE!

There was once a town on the side of the mountain. The mountain top was covered with beautiful snow which flowed crisp and clear to the river that supplied water to the people.

The river emptied into a lake near the bottom of the mountain. One day a local townsperson came to realize that the snow which supplied the river must surely run out as all the water continually flowed down to the lake. And the lake water evaporated into the air.

"We must save the water; the molecule is too valuable to waste!" he cried.

In a panic the town collected massive taxes to install a large pump that could be powered by burning the local trees and built a pipe to direct the lake water back to the top of the mountain. They also covered the lake to prevent evaporation.

The towns celebrated their wisdom and conservation of the water, feeling confident that not one molecule would be wasted.

Over the years, snow ceased to fall on the top of the mountain as there was no longer rain in the sky. The trees grew scarce as the town continued harvesting them to power the massive pump. And the water in the river and lake became more polluted.

The town was concerned. "What happened to our water?", the townspeople cried. "We have worked so hard to conserve this resource? We have spent all our money to recycle it, our trees have all been burnt to pump it up the mountain, so it can be reused, yet we can no longer drink our water."

THE SUSTAINABLE PLASTICS ECONOMY   TERESA CLARK

The town gathered together discussing new measures. Could they install a filter to clean the water? How could they lower the temperature on the mountain to prevent the little snow left from melting? What new materials could they use to power the pump? Would they need to move to a new mountain?

As the town continued deliberating, a wise man stepped forward. "You failed because you did not understand what you were trying to save." He continued to teach them of the circular process within nature. How the water changed form from ice, to water, into vapor and then back into the snow that fell on the mountain top and fed the river. They learned that the process of the water flowing to the lake, evaporating and returning to the mountain was the ultimate wisdom of nature; purifying the water and returning it to the mountain top without the need to burn trees.

The town needed to expand their understanding to the circular nature of water rather than focus only on the river.

Such is the dilemma of modern day sustainability. With the best of intentions, we attempt to circumvent natural processes without understanding the larger impacts. Most often the human understanding pales in comparison to the millennia of natures' processes. The Circular Economy and Sustainable Plastics Economy aim to harness the wisdom of nature and replicate it in human processes. Just as the town needed to expand their understanding of the river water, we must expand or understanding of plastics and how they fit into the carbon flows of nature. We do not need to protect a plastic molecule, the solution is understanding and integrating plastics into the broader circular process of carbon. This will achieve

Printed in Great Britain
by Amazon